Instant F
Cooker

50 INSTANT MOUTHWATERING
RECIPES FOR THE WHOLE FAMILY

By K. Connors

Table of Contents

Introduction

A lot of people hear about Instant Pots but have no idea how they're used! Well, an Instant Pot is basically a mash up of a rice cooker, pressure cooker, slow cooker, and other pots in one electric device. This is simply brilliant because the Instant Pot has all the advantages that those pots offer. For instance, the pressure cooker that cooks your food in a matter of minutes or the slow cooker that can take up to 12 hours to cook your food and give you a lot of free time. With the delicious 50 recipes that are offered in this book, your life really can't get much easier. Cooking with an Instant Pot is a huge advantage in itself, but there are four main reasons that make the Instant Pot a necessity in your house:

You will save time:

In my personal experience of cooking for 4 adults, I can say that I spend more than six hours each day in the kitchen doing everything from cooking to cleaning and washing the dishes. If you're someone who cooks a lot, you know that cooking can be quite messy even if you are preparing a simple salad. You always end up sticky and sweaty with a sink full of dishes to wash and no one to help. That's where the Instant Pot really comes in handy. Instead of spending more than six hours in the kitchen, you can lower that number to less than two, which is more than awesome.

A pot to use all year round for everything:

From enchiladas and soups to desserts and cakes - From winter to summer, the Instant Pot is a pot that you will use every day and every season!

Say goodbye to cleaning pots and pans:

Whether you're single or a mom, a man or a woman, I personally like to keep my nails clean. That doesn't happen when you have to scrub and clean pots every single day. Again, that's where your Instant Pot comes in handy because it is very easy to clean. Instead of cooking in two pots, a skillet and a saucepan, you'll need just one Instant Pot.

Cook in it all day:

You'll find out that the cooking time for all the recipes below are less than one hour on high pressure using the pressure cooker feature on the Instant Pot. This means you can have your meals prepared in a matter of minutes! There is also the feature of the slow cooker in the Instant Pot that enables you to cook your meals for hours while you do whatever you want. Some of the recipes below like the Apple Cider Roast Sandwich, Swedish Meatballs with Gravy, Pork and Mushroom Gravy, and Salsa Chicken you can cook for four to eight hours on low without having to check on them every minute.

Brown Lentils and Spinach Soup
(Prep Time: 5 min | Cooking Time: 12 min |
Servings 2 to 4)

Ingredients:

- 4 cups of baby spinach, sliced
- 4 cups of veggies broth
- 1 cup of brown lentils
- 2 carrots, diced
- 1 cup of yellow onion, diced

- 1 stalk of celery, diced
- 2 teaspoons of cumin
- 1 teaspoon of turmeric
- 2 cloves of garlic, minced
- ½ tablespoon of olive oil
- Black pepper
- Salt

Directions:

1. Heat the oil in a pressure cooker by pressing the sauté button.
2. Add the onion with celery, carrot and garlic, then cook them for 5 min.
3. Stir in the broth with lentils, some salt and pepper, then put on the lid and cook them for 13 min on high pressure.
4. Once the time is up, use the natural method to release the pressure.
5. Fold the spinach into the soup, then let it sit for 3 min.
6. Adjust the seasoning of the soup, then serve it warm and enjoy.

Instant Marinara Sauce

(Prep Time: 10 min | Cooking Time: 47 min |
Servings 6 cups)

Ingredients:

- 56 ounces of canned whole tomatoes, peeled
- 1 small yellow onion, finely chopped
- 2 tablespoons of olive oil
- 2 tablespoons of butter

- ½ tablespoon of dry oregano
- 4 cloves of garlic, minced
- Black pepper
- Salt

Directions:

1. Squeeze the tomato with your hands until it is well drained, then place it in a bowl.
2. Stir the butter with oil in a pressure cooker, then sauté the garlic in it for 1 min.
3. Stir in the drained tomato with the remaining ingredients, then put on the lid and cook for 46 min on high pressure.
4. Once the time is up, use the natural method to release the pressure.
5. Serve your marinara sauce right away or place it aside to cool down, then store in the fridge in tightly sealed jars or containers until ready to use and enjoy.

Glazed Turkey Meatballs

(Prep Time: 10 min | Cooking Time: 16 min | Servings 4)

Ingredients:

- 1 pound of lean turkey, minced
- 5 crackers, crushed
- ½ cup of soy sauce
- ¼ cup of green onions, thinly sliced
- ¼ cup of rice vinegar
- 3 tablespoons of buttermilk
- 3 tablespoons of brown sugar

- 3 tablespoons of canola oil
- 1 tablespoon of sesame seeds
- 1 tablespoon of cornstarch
- 2 teaspoons of fresh ginger, peeled and grated
- 1 clove of garlic, minced
- Black pepper
- Salt

Directions:

1. In a large mixing bowl, mix the crackers with turkey, buttermilk, onion, some salt and pepper with your hands to combine the flavors.
2. Shape the mix into bite size meatballs.
3. Pour 1 tablespoon of oil in the Instant Pot and press the sauté button to heat it.
4. Brown in it the meatballs for 3 min on each side.
5. In the meantime, whisk in it the soy sauce with vinegar, garlic, 2 tablespoons of canola oil and brown sugar, cornstarch, a pinch of salt and pepper to make the teriyaki sauce.
6. Pour the sauce all over the meatballs and stir them gently, then put on the lid and cook them for 12 min on high pressure.
7. Once the time is up, use the natural method to release the pressure, then serve your meatballs warm and enjoy.

Faux Chicken Pho

(Prep Time: 10 min | Cooking Time: 36 min | Servings 4)

Ingredients:

- 4 pounds of chicken, cut into pieces
- 1 head of bok choy, roughly chopped
- 2 yellow onions, peeled and quartered
- 1 daikon root, peeled and spiralized

- 1 inch of fresh ginger, peeled and grated
- 3 cloves
- 1 cup of fresh cilantro leaves
- 1 lemongrass stalk, sliced
- 1 tablespoon of coriander seeds
- 1 teaspoon of green cardamoms
- Black pepper
- Salt

Directions:

1. Place a small pan over medium heat and brown in it the coriander seeds for 7 min.
2. Transfer cilantro with chicken, coriander and other spices, lemongrass, and salt and pepper.
3. Place the lid and cook for 32 min over high pressure.
4. Once the time is up, use the fast method to release the pressure to make the broth.
5. Use a colander to strain the broth, then pour it back into the Instant Pot.
6. Stir in the daikon with bok choy then put on the lid and cook them for 7 min over high pressure.
7. Once the time is up, use the natural method to release the pressure.
8. Drain the chicken pieces and shred them, then stir them into the soup.
9. Adjust the seasoning of the soup, then serve it warm and enjoy.

Apple Cider Roast Sandwich

(Prep Time: 10 min | Cooking Time: 10 min |
Servings 4)

Ingredients:

- 2 pounds of beef roast, sliced
- 1 small red onion, peeled and sliced
- ½ cup of veggies broth
- 4 tablespoons of olive oil

- 1 tablespoon of lemon juice
- 1 tablespoon of dry parsley
- 2 cloves of garlic, minced
- 1 teaspoon of olive oil
- 1 teaspoon of apple cider vinegar
- Black pepper
- Salt

Directions:

1. Press the sauté button on the Instant Pot and heat the oil in it.
2. Combine in the meat with onion, garlic, lemon juice, parsley, some salt and pepper, then cook them for 6 min while stirring often.
3. Stir in the remaining ingredients, then put on the lid and cook them for 9 min over high pressure.
4. Once the time is up, use the natural method to release the pressure.
5. Drain the meat slices and place them in some bread pieces with your favorite toppings.
6. Serve your sandwiches warm and enjoy.

Chipotle Barbacoa

(Prep Time: 10 min | Cooking Time: 1 h 30 min |
Servings 6)

Ingredients:

- 3 pounds of chuck roast, sliced into chunks
- 4 ounces of canned chilies
- 1 yellow onion, peeled and thinly sliced
- ½ cup of water
- 3 chipotle peppers, dry and crushed
- Fresh juice of 3 limes
- 1 tablespoon of cumin

- 1 tablespoon of oregano
- 4 cloves of garlic, crushed
- Black pepper
- Salt

Directions:

1. Combine all the ingredients in an Instant Pot, then put on the lid and cook them for 1 hour with high pressure.
2. Once the time is up, drain the roast and shred it, then stir it back into the pot with the remaining broth.
3. Press the sauté button to let the roast cook until it absorbs most of the juices and it becomes moist. Then serve it warm and enjoy.

Nutty Quinoa
(Prep Time: 15 min | Cooking Time: 20 min | Servings 4)

Ingredients:

- 1 cup of quinoa
- 1 can of coconut milk
- The zest and juice of 1 lime, grated
- ¼ cup of water
- Salt

Directions:

1. Stir all the ingredients into an Instant Pot, then put on the lid and cook them for 1 min on high pressure.
2. Once the time is up, use the quick method to release the pressure.
3. Adjust the seasoning of the quinoa. Then serve it warm and enjoy.

Buffalo Meatballs Bites

(Prep Time: 10 min | Cooking Time: 20 min |
Servings 4)

Ingredients:

- 1 ½ pound of lean chicken, minced

- ¾ cup of almond meal
- 6 tablespoons of hot sauce
- 4 tablespoons of butter
- 2 tablespoons of ghee
- 2 small green onions, finely chopped
- 1 clove of garlic, minced
- Black pepper
- Salt

Directions:

1. Mix the chicken with almond meal, garlic, green onions, some salt and pepper in a large mixing bowl, then mix them well.
2. Shape the mix into small meatballs.
3. Heat the ghee in an Instant Pot, then brown in it the meatballs for 2 to 4 min.
4. Combine the butter with hot sauce in a small saucepan, then heat it through.
5. Pour the mix all over the meatballs, then put on the lid and cook them for 16 min over high heat.
6. Once the time is up, use the natural method to release the pressure. Then serve your saucy buffalo meatballs warm and enjoy.

Instant Shepherd Pie

(Prep Time: 15 min | Cooking Time: 28 min |
Servings 6)

Ingredients:

- 1-pound lean beef, minced
- 4 large red potatoes, peeled
- 3 carrots, sliced
- 1 cup of beef broth
- 1 cup of cheddar cheese, shredded
- 1 cup of green peas, frozen
- ½ cup of corn
- 1 yellow onion, diced
- 1 egg
- 3 tablespoons of flour
- 2 tablespoons of butter
- 1 teaspoon of garlic powder
- Black pepper
- Salt

Directions:

1. Stir the diced potato with 1 cup of water and some salt in Instant Pot.
2. Put on the lid and cook it for 8 min on high pressure.
3. Once the time is up, use the quick method to release the pressure.
4. Pour the potatoes into a colander and let them dry and cool down.
5. Transfer the potato to a large mixing bowl, then combine the egg, 2 tablespoons of butter, garlic powder and some salt.

6. Mix them well with a potato masher, then place the mix aside.
7. Press the sauté button on the Instant Pot, then brown in it the beef for 6 min.
8. Combine in the onion with carrots, peas, corn, some salt and pepper then cook them for 2 min.
9. Whisk the broth in a mixing bowl with flour, then stir it into the pot.
10. Put on the lid and spread the mix in the pot.
11. Spread the potato on top of the beef mix, then put the lid and cook them for 12 min over high pressure.
12. Once the time is up, use the quick method to release the pressure. Serve your shepherd pie warm with the cheese on top and enjoy.

French Style Dipping Sandwiches

(Prep Time: 15 min | Cooking Time: 38 min | Servings 8)

Ingredients:

- 3.5 pounds of beef rump roast
- 3 cups of beef broth
- 8 hoagies rolls
- 4 tablespoons of butter
- 2 tablespoons of brown sugar

- 2 tablespoons of Worcestershire sauce
- 1 tablespoon of balsamic vinegar
- 2 teaspoons of onion flakes
- 2 teaspoons of paprika
- 2 teaspoons of mustard powder
- 2 teaspoons of garlic powder
- Black pepper
- Salt

Directions:

1. Slice the roast into large dices, then toss it in a large bowl with the brown sugar, onion flakes, paprika, mustard, garlic powder, some salt and pepper.
2. Transfer them into an Instant Pot.
3. Stir in the vinegar with Worcestershire sauce and broth.
4. Put on the lid and cook the roast for 38 min over high pressure.
5. Once the time is up, use the quick method to release the pressure.
6. Spread the butter over the hoagies slices.
7. Drain the roast slices and shred them. Then divide them on the hoagies rolls and serve them warm with your favorite dip.

Creamy Tikka Masala

(Prep Time: 15 min | Cooking Time: 20 min | Servings 4)

Ingredients:

- 1½ pound of chicken, diced
- 28 ounces of tomato, diced
- ¾ cup of heavy cream
- 1 yellow onion, diced
- 2 tablespoons of tomato paste
- 1 tablespoon of garam masala

- 2 teaspoons of paprika
- 1 teaspoon of olive oil
- 2 cloves of garlic, minced
- Black pepper
- Salt

Directions:

1. Press the sauté button on the Instant Pot, then heat the oil in it.
2. Add the garlic with onion and cook them for 4 min.
3. Stir in the remaining ingredients, then put on the lid and cook them for 16 min over high pressure.
4. Serve your tikka masala warm and enjoy.

Beef and Broccoli Stew

(Prep Time: 15 min | Cooking Time: 30 min |
Servings 4)

Ingredients:

- 2 ½ pounds of flank steak, cut into strips
- 1 pound of broccoli florets
- ¾ cup of soy sauce
- ½ cup of beef broth
- 1 small yellow onion, diced

- 3 dry red chilies, crushed
- 2 tablespoons of potato starch
- 4 cloves of garlic, minced
- 2 tablespoons of fish sauce
- 1 ½ tablespoon of sesame oil
- Black pepper
- Salt

Directions:

1. Stir 1 tablespoon of sesame oil with soy sauce, chilies and fish sauce in a large mixing bowl, then stir in the flank steak strips and let them sit for 15 min.
2. Heat the remaining oil in the Instant Pot by pressing the sauté button.
3. Add the onion and cook it for 3 min.
4. Stir in the steak mix and cook them for 3 min.
5. Combine in the broth with some salt and pepper, then put on the lid and cook them for 12 min over high pressure.
6. Spoon some of the liquid from the stew into a mixing bowl then add the starch and whisk them until no lumps are found.
7. Pour the mix into the pot with the broccoli. Press the sauté button and let them cook for 8 to 10 min.
8. Once the time is up, and the broccoli is done, serve your stew warm and enjoy.

Saucy Beef Macaroni

(Prep Time: 10 min | Cooking Time: 14 min |
Servings 4 to 6)

Ingredients:

- 1 pound of lean beef, minced
- 1 pound of macaroni
- 24 ounces of tomato, pureed
- 15 ounces of tomato sauce
- 2 ½ cup of water
- ½ onion, diced

- ¼ cup of dry wine
- 1 tablespoon of Worcestershire sauce
- 1 tablespoon of olive oil
- 2 teaspoons of dry basil
- 2 cloves of garlic, minced
- Black pepper
- Salt

Directions:

1. Press the sauté button on the Instant Pot then heat the oil in it.
2. Sauté in it the meat for 5 min.
3. Add the garlic with onion and cook them for 2 min.
4. Stir in the remaining ingredients, then put on the lid and cook them for 6 min on high pressure.
5. Once the time is up, use the quick method to release the pressure.
6. Serve your beef macaroni warm and enjoy.

Pork and Mushroom Gravy

(Prep Time: 15 min | Cooking Time: 20 min | Servings 4)

Ingredients:

- 4 thick pork chops
- 8 ounces of baby mushroom, sliced
- 1 ¼ cup of broth
- 1 cup of milk

- ½ cup of yellow onion, thinly sliced
- 2 tablespoons of olive oil
- 3 tablespoons of cornstarch
- 1 ½ tablespoon of butter
- Black pepper
- Salt

Directions:

1. Combine the butter with milk, 1 tablespoon of starch and some salt in a mixing bowl well to make the gravy.
2. Season the pork chops with some salt and pepper.
3. Press the sauté button on the Instant Pot, then heat the oil in it.
4. Add the pork chops and brown them for 2 to 3 min on each side.
5. Drain the chops and place them aside.
6. Add the onion with garlic to the pot and cook it for 2 min.
7. Stir in the gravy mix with broth, pork chops, mushroom, some salt and pepper.
8. Replace the lid and cook for 9 min on high pressure.
9. Once the time is up, use the natural method to release the pressure.
10. Spoon some of the liquid into a mixing bowl, then add the cornstarch and mix them well.
11. Pour the mix into the pot then press the sauté button and cook for 5 to 7 min or until the gravy

becomes slightly thick. Then serve it warm and enjoy.

Sunny Chicken Skillet

(Prep Time: 15 min | Cooking Time: 20 min |
Servings 4 to 6)

Ingredients:

- 2 pounds of chicken breasts, halved
- 1 cup of spinach, sliced
- ¾ cup of heavy cream
- ½ cup of chicken broth
- ½ cup of oily sun-dried tomatoes, drained and sliced

- ½ cup of parmesan cheese
- 2 tablespoons of olive oil
- 2 teaspoons of Italian seasoning
- 3 cloves of garlic, minced
- Black pepper
- Salt

Directions:

1. Toss the chicken breasts with oil, garlic, Italian seasoning, and some salt and pepper in a large mixing bowl.
2. Press the sauté button on the Instant Pot and let it heat up for a while.
3. Pour into it the chicken mix, then sauté them for 3 min on each side.
4. Add the broth and put on the lid then cook them for 4 min on high pressure.
5. Once the time is up, use the quick method to release the pressure.
6. Stir in the cream with some salt and pepper, then let them cook for 6 min.
7. Combine in the cheese and let it cook until it melts.
8. Fold in the tomato with spinach, then keep sautéing for another 3 min until they are done.
9. Serve your sunny chicken warm with some pasta and enjoy.

The Perfect Greek Yogurt

(Prep Time: 15 min | Cooking Time: 10 h | Servings 14)

Ingredients:

- 16 cups of milk
- 2 tablespoons of plain yogurt

Directions:

1. Pour the milk into an Instant Pot, then put on the lid and click the boil button.
2. Cook the milk for few minutes, then whisk it and cover it again.
3. When the pot starts beeping, whisk it again and test it with a thermometer to ensure the temperature reaches 180 degrees F.
4. If it does, turn off the Instant Pot. If still under the temperature, click the sauté button and let cook for a few minutes before testing it again while whisking all the time.
5. Fill the sink with some cold water then place the pot of milk in it.
6. Keep whisking the milk until the temperature reaches 95 to 110 degrees.
7. Pour some of the milk in a mixing bowl, then add the yogurt and mix them well.
8. Pour the mix back into the pot with the remaining milk.
9. Put on the lid and press the yogurt button on the Instant Pot, then adjust the timer to 8 min.
10. Once the time is up, turn off the Instant Pot and place it in the fridge for 6 to 7 hours or until the yogurt cools down completely and thickens.
11. Serve your yogurt with some cut up fruit and enjoy.

Herbed Lemon Breasts

(Prep Time: 10 min | Cooking Time: 16 min | Servings 4)

Ingredients:

- 1 ½ pound of chicken breasts, halved
- ½ cup of chicken broth
- The juice of 1 lemon
- ¼ cup of white cooking wine
- 1 medium yellow onion diced

- 1 tablespoon of ghee
- 4 cloves of garlic, minced
- 1 tablespoon of parsley, finely chopped
- 1 tablespoon of arrow root flour
- Black pepper
- Salt

Directions:

1. Press the sauté button on the Instant Pot, then melt the ghee in it.
2. Add the onion and cook it for 6 min.
3. Stir in the rest of the ingredients except for the flour, then put on the lid and cook them for 16 min on high pressure.
4. Once the time is up, use the natural method to release the pressure.
5. Spoon some of the liquid into a small mixing bowl, then add the arrow root flour and whisk them well.
6. Stir the mix into the pot and press the sauté button, then let it cook for 4 min until the sauce thickens.
7. Serve your lemon chicken warm with some rice or pasta and enjoy.

Pot Roasted Baby Potatoes

(Prep Time: 10 min | Cooking Time: 11 min |
Servings 6)

Ingredients:

- 2 ½ pounds of baby potatoes
- Black pepper
- Salt

Directions:

1. Pour 1 cup of water into an Instant Pot, then lower into it a steamer rack.
2. Place the potatoes in the rack, then put on the lid and cook them for 11 min on high pressure.
3. Once the time is up, use the natural method to release the pressure.
4. Transfer the potato to a large mixing bowl, then toss it with some salt and pepper and herbs if you desire, then serve it warm and enjoy.

Saucy ketchup Chicken Bites

(Prep Time: 10 min | Cooking Time: 20 min |
Servings 4)

Ingredients:

- 1 ½ pound of chicken, diced
- 1 cup of honey
- ½ cup of white onion, diced
- ½ cup of soy sauce
- ¼ cup of ketchup
- 3 tablespoons of water

- 2 tablespoons of vegetable oil
- 1 tablespoon of cornstarch
- 1 teaspoon of garlic, minced
- Black pepper
- Salt

Directions:

1. Combine the chicken with honey, onion, soy sauce, ketchup, garlic, some salt and pepper in an Instant Pot.
2. Put on the lid and cook them for 16 min on high pressure.
3. Once the time is up, use the natural method to release the pressure.
4. Mix the cornstarch with water in a small bowl.
5. Stir the mix into the pot with the chicken, then press the sauté button and let it cook for 4 min until the sauce thickens.
6. Serve your saucy chicken warm and enjoy.

Cheesy Steak Burger

(Prep Time: 10 min | Cooking Time: 9 min |
Servings 4)

Ingredients:

- 1 ½ cup of lean beef steak, minced
- 4 burger buns

- 2 ½ cup of onion, thinly sliced
- 2 cups of mozzarella cheese
- 10.5 ounces of onion soup
- 1 cup of baby mushroom, diced
- ¾ cup of bell pepper, diced
- 2 cloves of garlic, minced
- Black pepper
- Salt

Directions:

1. Stir the onion with beef, bell pepper, onion soup, garlic, and some salt and pepper in an Instant Pot.
2. Put on the lid and cook them for 9 min on high pressure.
3. Once the time is up, use the natural method to release the pressure.
4. Stir in the cheese, then spoon the mix into the buns and serve them hot.

Mexican Style Chicken Tacos

(Prep Time: 15 min | Cooking Time: 20 min | Servings 6)

Ingredients:

- 2 pounds of chicken breasts, boneless and skinless
- 14.5 ounces of tomato, finely chopped
- ½ cup of salsa, mild
- 1 can of green chilies, drained
- 4 tablespoons of brown sugar
- 1 tablespoon of olive oil

- 1 tablespoon of chili powder
- 1 tablespoon of cumin
- 1 teaspoon of garlic powder
- ½ teaspoon of dry oregano
- ½ teaspoon of paprika
- Black pepper
- Salt

Directions:

1. Stir all the ingredients into an Instant Pot with some salt and pepper.
2. Put on the lid and cook them for 25 min on high pressure.
3. Once the time is up, use the quick method to release the pressure.
4. Drain the chicken breasts and shredded, then stir them back into the pot.
5. Spoon the shredded chicken mix into taco shells or tortillas, then serve them with your favorite toppings and enjoy.

Salsa Chicken

(Prep Time: 15 min | Cooking Time: 26 min |
Servings 4 to 6)

Ingredients:

- 2 pounds of chicken breasts
- 16 ounces of salsa verde

- 1 teaspoon of paprika
- 1 teaspoon of cumin
- Black pepper
- Salt

Directions:

1. Stir all the ingredients into an Instant Pot, then put on the lid and cook them for 26 min on high pressure.
2. Once the time is up, use the natural method to release the pressure.
3. Drain the chicken breasts and shred them, then stir them back into the pot.
4. Serve our salsa chicken warm and enjoy.

Sweet Sesame and Orange Chicken

(Prep Time: 10 min | Cooking Time: 10 min | Servings 4)

Ingredients:

- 4 chicken breasts, diced
- ½ cup of fresh orange juice
- 1/3 cup of soy sauce
- ¼ cup of brown sugar
- ¼ cup of water
- 4 tablespoons of water
- 2 tablespoons of ketchup
- 1 tablespoons of apple cider vinegar

- 1 tablespoon of cornstarch
- Sesame seeds
- Black pepper
- Salt

Directions:

1. Whisk the water with cornstarch in a small bowl and place it aside.
2. Stir the remaining ingredients into an Instant Pot, then put on the lid and cook them for 6 min on high pressure.
3. Once the time is up, use the natural method to release the pressure.
4. Stir in the cornstarch and water mix, then press the sauté button on the pot.
5. Cook the orange chicken for 2 to 4 min until it thickens, then serve it warm with sesame seeds and enjoy.

Glazed Peanut Chicken

(Prep Time: 10 min | Cooking Time: 25 min |
Servings 4 to 6)

Ingredients:

- 6 to 8 chicken thighs, boneless and diced
- 1 cup of peanuts
- ¼ cup of flour

- 6 tablespoons of soy sauce
- 6 tablespoons of rice vinegar
- 3 tablespoons of water
- 2 tablespoons of honey
- 1 tablespoon of cornstarch
- 1 tablespoon of vegetable oil
- 3 cloves of garlic, minced
- Black pepper
- Salt

Directions:

1. Toss the chicken dices with flour, some salt, and pepper in a large mixing bowl.
2. Press the sauté button on the Instant Pot and heat the oil in it.
3. Sauté half of the chicken for 4 min then drain it and place it aside.
4. Add the remaining chicken and sauté it for another 4 min.
5. Stir in the browned chicken on the side with garlic, then put on the lid and cook it for 1 min on low pressure.
6. Whisk the soy sauce with vinegar, honey and cornstarch in a mixing bowl to make the sauce.
7. Stir the mix into the pot, then press the sauté button and let it cook for few minutes until the sauce thickens.

8. Fold the peanuts into the saucy chicken, then serve it warm and enjoy.

Chicken Dumplings Soup

(Prep Time: 15 min | Cooking Time: 20 min |
Servings 4)

Ingredients:

- 1 ½ pounds of chicken thighs, boneless and skinless
- 6 cups of chicken stock
- 1 ¾ cup of Bisquick baking mix
- 1 cup green peas, frozen
- 1 cup of carrots shredded

- 2/3 cup of milk
- 1 small white onion, diced
- ¼ cup of heavy cream
- 3 tablespoons of butter
- 1 teaspoon of dry thyme
- ½ teaspoon of poultry seasoning
- Black pepper
- Salt

Directions:

1. Season the chicken thighs with some salt and pepper.
2. Press the sauté button on the Instant Pot, then melt the butter in it.
3. Add the onion with carrot and peas, then cook them for 2 min.
4. Combine the chicken with stock, thyme, poultry seasoning, some salt and pepper.
5. Put on the lid and cook them for 12 min on high pressure.
6. Once the time is up, use the natural method to release the pressure.
7. Drain the chicken thighs gently and shred them, then stir them back into the pot.
8. Mix the baking mix with milk in a mixing bowl until you get a smooth dough.
9. Use a large tablespoon to scoop the dough and place it on the soup.

10. Press the sauté button on the Instant Pot, then let the soup cook for 9 min until the dumplings are done.
11. Once the time is up, add the heavy cream to the soup and stir it gently, then adjust the seasoning of the soup.
12. Serve your soup warm and enjoy.

Sticky Brown Chicken

(Prep Time: 15 min | Cooking Time: 20 min | Servings 4 to 6)

Ingredients:

- 2 pounds of chicken breasts, skinless and boneless
- 1 cup of brown sugar
- 2/3 cup of apple cider vinegar
- 1/3 cup of lemon lime soda

- 2 tablespoons of water
- 2 tablespoons of cornstarch
- 2 tablespoons of soy sauce
- 3 cloves of garlic, minced
- Black pepper
- Salt

Directions:

1. Mix the vinegar with soda, sugar, garlic and soy sauce in a small mixing bowl to make the sauce.
2. Season the chicken breasts with some salt and pepper, then stir them into an Instant Pot with the sauce.
3. Put on the lid and cook the chicken for 20 min on high pressure.
4. Once the time is up, drain the chicken breasts and place them aside to lose heat.
5. Mix the water with cornstarch in a small bowl, then stir into the sauce in the pot.
6. Press the sauté button and cook the sauce until it becomes slightly thick.
7. Shred the chicken and stir into the pot with the sauce, then serve it warm and enjoy.

Cheesy Chicken Breasts

(Prep Time: 15 min | Cooking Time: 24 min | Servings 4)

Ingredients:

- 1 pound of chicken breasts
- 16 ounces of tomato sauce
- 1 1/3 cup of mozzarella cheese, shredded
- 1/3 cup of parmesan cheese, grated
- 1/3 cup of olive oil
- 1 1/3 tablespoon of butter, melted

- Garlic powder
- Black pepper
- Salt

Directions:

1. Season the chicken breasts with some garlic powder, salt and pepper.
2. Press the sauté button on the Instant Pot, then heat the oil in it.
3. Sauté in it the chicken breasts for 3 to 4 min on each side.
4. Divide the button on the chicken breasts, then top them with the tomato sauce and parmesan cheese.
5. Put on the lid and cook them for 16 min on high pressure.
6. Once the time is up, use the quick method to release the pressure.
7. Sprinkle the mozzarella cheese over the chicken breasts, then put on the lid and let them sit for 6 min until the cheese melts.
8. Serve your cheesy chicken breasts warm with some pasta and enjoy.

Cola Roast

(Prep Time: 10 min | Cooking Time: 20 min |
Servings 6)

Ingredients:

- 3 ½ pound of beef roast

- 1 cup of coca cola
- 5 Pepperoncini peppers
- 1 packet of au jus gravy mix
- 1 packet of ranch dressing powder
- 4 tablespoons of butter
- 2 tablespoons of oil
- 2 tablespoons of milk
- 2 tablespoons of cornstarch
- Black pepper
- Salt

Directions:

1. Press the sauté button on the Instant Pot and heat the oil in it.
2. Add the roast and brown it for 3 to 5 min on each side.
3. Stir the cola with the peppers, ranch dressing, butter, gravy mix, and salt and pepper into the pot then put on the lid and cook them for 16 min on high pressure.
4. Once the time is up, use the natural method to release the pressure.
5. Drain the roast and place it aside.
6. Mix the cornstarch with milk in a small bowl, then stir it into the liquid in the pot.
7. Press the sauté button and cook the sauce until it thickens slightly.

8. Serve your roast warm and enjoy.

Steak Gravy
(Prep Time: 10 min | Cooking Time: 10 min |
Servings 2 to 4)

Ingredients:

- 1 ½ pound of beef steak, diced
- 1 cup of baby mushroom, sliced
- 10 ounces of French onion soup
- 10 ounces of water

- 1 packet of au jus gravy mix
- 2 tablespoons of cornstarch
- Black pepper
- Salt

Directions:

1. Stir the steak with mushroom, onion soup, water, gravy mix, some salt and pepper.
2. Put on the lid and cook them for 5 min on high pressure.
3. Once the time is up, use the natural method to release the pressure.
4. Spoon some of the sauce from the pot into a small mixing bowl.
5. Add the cornstarch and mix them well.
6. Stir the mix back into the pot, then press the sauté button and let it cook for few minutes until it thickens slightly.
7. Serve your steak gravy and mushroom warm and enjoy.

Classic Smoked Pot Roast

(Prep Time: 10 min | Cooking Time: 35 min |
Servings 4)

Ingredients:

- 1 ½ pound beef roast
- 2 cups of beef broth
- 2 tablespoons of brown sugar
- 1 tablespoon of liquid smoke
- 1 teaspoon of mustard powder
- 1 teaspoon of onion powder
- 2 fresh sprigs of thyme

- Black pepper
- Salt

Directions:

1. Mix the onion powder with mustard, sugar, some salt and pepper.
2. Rub the mix into the roast and place it in an Instant Pot.
3. Stir in the broth with liquid smoke and thyme, then put on the lid and cook it for 35 min on high pressure.
4. Once the time is up, use the natural method to release the pressure.
5. Serve your roast warm with some veggies and enjoy.

Dr. Pepper's Special Pork Roast

(Prep Time: 10 min | Cooking Time: 55 min |
Servings 8 to 10)

Ingredients:

- 4 pounds pork roast, sliced into large chunks
- 2 cups of Dr pepper soda
- 2 cups of favorite barbecue roast
- 1 yellow onion, thinly sliced
- 1 tablespoon of onion powder
- 1 tablespoon of garlic powder

- Black pepper
- Salt

Directions:

1. Season the roast garlic powder, onion powder, some salt and pepper.
2. Spread the onion in the Instant Pot then place the roast on it followed by the soda and barbecue sauce.
3. Put on the lid and cook the roast for 55 min on high pressure.
4. Once the time is up, use the natural method to release the pressure.
5. Serve your saucy roast warm and enjoy.

Hot Cheesy Sausage and Mac

(Prep Time: 15 min | Cooking Time: 6 min |
Servings 4)

Ingredients:

- 1 lean pound of sausages, loose
- 2 cups of macaroni
- 2 cups of water
- 15 ounces of tomato sauce
- 1 yellow onion, diced

- 1 cup of shredded Mexican cheese
- 1 tablespoon of oil
- 2 cloves of garlic, minced
- Black pepper
- Salt

Directions:

1. Combine the sausage with macaroni, water, tomato sauce, onion, oil, garlic, some salt and pepper in an Instant Pot.
2. Put on the lid and cook them for 6 min on high pressure.
3. Once the time is up, use the natural method to release the pressure.
4. Stir in the cheese into the macaroni then serve it warm and enjoy.

Sweet and Salty Short Ribs

(Prep Time: 10 min | Cooking Time: 23 min |
Servings 4)

Ingredients:

- 2 pounds of short ribs
- 1 cup of vinegar
- ½ cup of soy sauce
- 1/3 cup of brown sugar
- 4 cloves of garlic, crushed
- 3 bay leaves
- 2 tablespoons of oil

- 1 tablespoon of cornstarch
- 1 tablespoon of water
- Black pepper
- Salt

Directions:

1. Press the sauté button on the Instant Pot, then heat the oil in it.
2. Sauté in it the short ribs for 6 min while turning them often.
3. Stir in the sugar with garlic, vinegar, soy sauce, some salt and pepper.
4. Put on the lid and cook them for 16 min on high pressure.
5. Once the time is up, use the natural method to release the pressure.
6. Mix the cornstarch with water in a small bowl.
7. Stir the mix into the pot and press the sauté button.
8. Let the ribs cook for 7 min until the sauce thickens slightly, then serve it warm and enjoy.

Turkey Mozzarella Lasagna

(Prep Time: 15 min | Cooking Time: 22 min | Servings 4 to 6)

Ingredients:

- 1 pound of lean turkey, minced
- 1 large container of chunky tomato salsa
- 15 ounces of ricotta cheese
- 10 ounces of frozen spinach, thawed
- 6 lasagna noodles
- 1 ½ cup of mozzarella cheese, shredded
- 1 cup of water

- 1 teaspoon of Italian seasoning
- Black pepper
- Salt

Directions:

1. Combine the lean turkey with Italian seasoning in a large skillet, then cook for 9 min.
2. Mix the spinach with ricotta and 1 cup of mozzarella cheese, a pinch of salt and pepper in a large mixing bowl.
3. Grease a round dish that fits in your Instant Pot with some oil.
4. Cover the bottom of the dish with tomato salsa, then top it with ½ of the noodles followed by ½ of the browned turkey, some tomato salsa and ½ of the cheese mix.
5. Repeat the process to make another layer ending with tomato sauce on top.
6. Sprinkle the remaining mozzarella cheese on top.
7. Pour 1 cup of water into the Instant Pot, then lower a trivet into it and place the lasagna dish on top.
8. Put on the lid and cook the lasagna for 22 min on high pressure.
9. Once the time is up, use the quick method to release the pressure, then serve it warm and enjoy.

Spicy Chorizo Chili

(Prep Time: 10 min | Cooking Time: 22 min | Servings 4 to 6)

Ingredients:

- 2 pounds of lean beef, minced
- 7 ounces of chorizo, peeled and diced
- 1 yellow onion, finely chopped
- 2 cups of tomato, finely chopped
- 1 red chili, diced
- 1 carrot, diced

- 1 stalk of celery, diced
- 4 tablespoons of tomato paste
- 1 ½ tablespoon of olive oil
- 1 tablespoon of soy sauce
- 2 teaspoons of cumin
- 2 cloves of garlic, minced
- Black pepper
- Salt

Directions:

1. Press the sauté button on the Instant Pot, then heat the oil in it.
2. Add the carrot with onion, chili and celery, then cook them for 3 min.
3. Add the chorizo with beef and garlic, then cook them for another 3 min.
4. Stir in the remaining ingredients, then put on the lid and cook them for 16 min on high pressure.
5. Once the time is up, use the natural method to release the pressure then serve your chili warm and enjoy.

Instant Mashed Cauli-Potato

(Prep Time: 10 min | Cooking Time: 4 min |
Servings 4)

Ingredients:

- 1 head of cauliflower, roughly chopped
- 1 cup of water
- ¼ teaspoon of garlic powder
- Salt

Directions:

1. Pour 1 cup of water into an Instant Pot, then lower a trivet and basket into it.
2. Place the cauliflower in the basket, then put on the lid and cook it for 4 min on high pressure.
3. Once the time is up, use the natural method to release the pressure.
4. Transfer the cauliflower to a large mixing bowl.
5. Add to it some salt, butter and garlic powder.
6. Mash the mix well until it becomes smooth then serve it and enjoy.

Philly Cheese Steak Rolls

(Prep Time: 15 min | Cooking Time: 40 min |
Servings 6)

Ingredients:

- 2 ½ pound steak, sliced
- 6 slices of provolone cheese
- 6 hoagie rolls

- 1 large yellow onion, thinly sliced
- 1 cup of water
- 1 packet of dry Italian dressing mix
- 1 beef bouillon cube
- 2 cloves of garlic, minced
- Black pepper
- Salt

Directions:

1. Stir the steak with onion, water, Italian dressing, bouillon cube, garlic, some salt and pepper.
2. Put on the lid and cook them for 40 min on high pressure.
3. Once the time is up, use the natural method to release the pressure.
4. Divide the steak mix between the hoagie rolls, then top them with the provolone cheese slices.
5. Serve your sandwiches warm and enjoy.

Saucy Pulled Steak

(Prep Time: 15 min | Cooking Time: 36 min |
Servings 4)

Ingredients:

- 1 ½ pound flank steak, cut into chunks
- 3 cups of water
- 2 red bell peppers, sliced
- 1 cup of dry red wine
- 1 cup of tomato sauce

- ½ cup of green olives, pitted and halved
- 1/3 cup of canola oil
- 2 bay leaves
- 3 cloves of garlic, minced
- ½ teaspoon of cumin
- Black pepper
- Salt

Directions:

1. Stir all the ingredients into an Instant Pot, then put on the lid and cook them for 36 min on high pressure.
2. Once the time is up, use the natural method to release the pressure.
3. Drain the steak chunks from the sauce and shred it then stir it back into the pot.
4. Adjust the seasoning of the saucy steak, then serve it warm and enjoy.

Sticky Pineapple Chicken

(Prep Time: 10 min | Cooking Time: 13 min |
Servings 4)

Ingredients:

- 2 pounds of chicken breasts

- 8 ounces of pineapple, crushed
- ¾ cup of barbecue sauce
- Black pepper
- Salt

Directions:

1. Stir all the ingredients into an Instant Pot, then put on the lid and cook them for 13 min on high pressure.
2. Once the time is up, use the natural method to release the pressure.
3. Drain the chicken breasts and shred them, then stir them back into the pot.
4. Press the sauté button on the pot and let it cook until the sauce thickens, then serve it warm and enjoy.

Creamy Golden Potato Soup

(Prep Time: 15 min | Cooking Time: 20 min |
Servings 6 to 8)

Ingredients:

- 5 pounds of golden potato, peeled and cut into chunks
- 5 ½ cups of chicken broth
- 2 cups of cheddar cheese, shredded
- 1 ½ cup of milk
- 1 small shallot, minced

- 1/3 cup of sour cream
- 1/3 cup of cream cheese, softened
- 4 tablespoons of butter
- Black pepper
- Salt

Directions:

1. Stir the potato with shallot and broth into an Instant Pot.
2. Put on the lid and cook them for 11 min on high pressure.
3. Once the time is up, use the natural method to release the pressure.
4. Stir the remaining ingredients into the soup until the cheese melts.
5. Serve your soup hot right away or blend it smooth and enjoy.

Creamy Spinach Dip

(Prep Time: 10 min | Cooking Time: 5 min | Servings 6)

Ingredients:

- 16 ounces of parmesan cheese, shredded
- 14 ounces of artichoke hearts, drained
- 10 ounces of spinach, frozen and thawed

- 8 ounces of cream cheese
- 8 ounces of mozzarella cheese, shredded
- ½ cup of sour cream
- ½ cup of chicken broth
- ½ cup of mayo
- 1 teaspoon of onion powder
- 2 cloves of garlic, minced
- Black pepper
- Salt

Directions:

1. Combine the artichoke hearts with broth, garlic and mayo, sour cream, spinach, onion powder, some salt and pepper.
2. Put on the lid and cook them for 5 min on high pressure.
3. Once the time is up, use the natural method to release the pressure.
4. Stir the cheese into the mix until it melts, then serve your dip with crackers and enjoy.

Cajun Veggies Rice

(Prep Time: 10 min | Cooking Time: 14 min |
Servings 4)

Ingredients:

- 1 ½ cup of rice
- 1 red bell pepper, sliced
- 1 green bell pepper, sliced
- 1 yellow pepper, sliced
- 1 large carrot, sliced
- 2 ¼ cup of chicken broth

- 1 small onion, diced
- 1 tablespoon of oil
- 1 tablespoon of tomato paste
- 2 teaspoons of Cajun seasoning
- 2 cloves of garlic, minced
- Black pepper
- Salt

Directions:

1. Press the sauté button on the Instant Pot, then heat the oil in it.
2. Sauté the veggies in the oil for 4 min.
3. Stir in the remaining ingredients, then put on the lid and cook them for 10 min on high pressure.
4. Once the time is up, use the quick method to release the pressure.
5. Put the lid on and let the Cajun rice sit for 5 min, then serve it warm and enjoy.

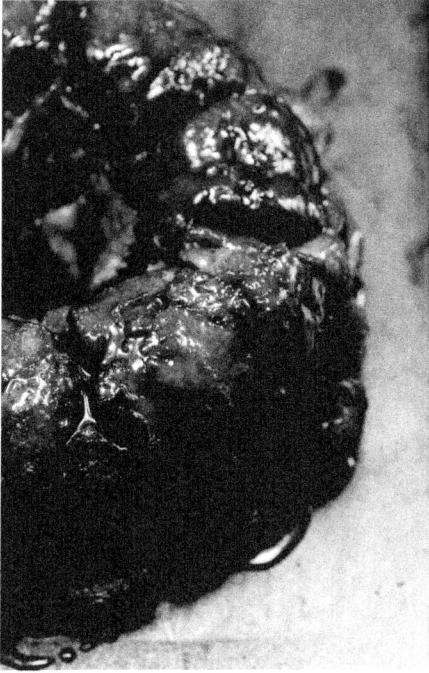

Vanilla Biscuits Cake
(Prep Time: 10 min | Cooking Time: 22 min |
Servings 6 to 8)

Ingredients:

- 2 packets of biscuit dough

- 1 ½ cup of water
- ½ cup of butter
- ½ cup of brown sugar
- 1 tablespoon of cinnamon
- ½ teaspoon of vanilla extract

Directions:

1. Pour the water into an Instant Pot, then lower a trivet into the pot.
2. Combine half of the brown sugar with the biscuit dough and cinnamon in a large zip lock bag.
3. Shake them roughly until the biscuit bites are coated with the sugar and cinnamon.
4. Place the biscuit dough in a greased baking pan that will fit in your Instant Pot, then place it on the trivet.
5. Put on the lid and cook the cake for 22 min on high pressure.
6. Once the time is up, use the quick method to release the pressure.
7. Add the vanilla with butter and brown sugar into a small, heavy pan. Then stir them until they melt.
8. Transfer the cake to a serving plate and pour the butter sauce over it, then serve it and enjoy.

Barbecue Bacon Meatloaf

(Prep Time: 10 min | Cooking Time: 21 min |
Servings 4 to 6)

Ingredients:

- 1 pound of lean beef, minced
- 6 bacon slices, finely chopped
- 2 cups of water
- ¼ cup of barbecue sauce
- ¼ cup of Italian bread crumbs
- ¼ cup of sour cream

- ¼ cup of barbecue sauce
- ¼ cup of milk
- 1 egg
- 1 tablespoon of Worcestershire sauce
- 1 teaspoon of garlic powder
- 1 clove of garlic, minced
- Black pepper
- Salt

Directions:

1. Pour the water into an Instant Pot, then place a trivet in it.
2. Combine all the ingredients in a large mixing bowl, then mix them well.
3. Transfer the mix to a lined baking dish that fits in your Instant Pot and shape it into a meatloaf.
4. Place the dish on the trivet and put on the lid, then cook it for 21 min on high pressure.
5. Once the time is up, use the quick method to release the pressure.
6. Serve your meatloaf warm with some extra barbecue sauce and enjoy.

Swedish Meatballs with Gravy

(Prep Time: 15 min | Cooking Time: 30 min | Servings 4)

Ingredients:

- 1 pound of lean beef, minced
- 14.5 ounces of beef broth
- 1 packet of French onion soup
- 1 cup of heavy cream

- ½ cup of bread crumbs
- ½ cup of baby mushroom, diced
- ½ cup of sour cream
- ½ yellow onion, diced
- 1 egg
- 6 tablespoons of cornstarch
- 5 tablespoons of butter, melted
- 2 tablespoons of Worcestershire sauce
- 1 tablespoon of Dijon mustard
- 1 tablespoon of olive oil
- Black pepper
- Salt

Directions:

1. Combine the beef with egg, onion soup, bread crumbs, 1 tablespoon of Worcestershire sauce, salt and pepper in a large mixing bowl.
2. Mix them well, then shape the mix into bite-sized meatballs.
3. Press the sauté button on the on the Instant Pot, then heat the oil in it.
4. Sauté the meatballs for 2 to 3 min on each side.
5. Stir in the onions and cook them for 3 min.
6. Mix the sour cream with 3 tablespoons of cornstarch, broth, heavy cream and Worcestershire sauce, Dijon mustard, butter, some salt and pepper in a large mixing bowl until no lumps are found.

7. Stir the mix into the pot with the meatballs and mushroom, then replace the lid and cook them for 19 min on high pressure.
8. Once the time is up, use the natural method to release the pressure.
9. Use a slotted spoon to drain the meatballs and place them aside.
10. Add the rest of the cornstarch to the pot with the remaining liquid and mix them well until there are no lumps.
11. Stir the meatballs back into the pot and press the sauté button, then cook it until the sauce thickens.
12. Serve your Swedish meatballs and gravy warm and enjoy.

Cheesy Mac and Ham

(Prep Time: 10 min | Cooking Time: 11 min | Servings 6)

Ingredients:

- 16 ounces of macaroni
- 3 cups of ham, cooked and diced
- 3 cups of chicken broth
- 2 cups of milk
- ½ cup of white onion, diced
- ½ cup of parmesan cheese

- ¼ cup of flour
- 1 tablespoon of olive oil
- ½ teaspoon of dry parsley
- ½ teaspoon of dry basil
- 2 cloves of garlic, minced
- Black pepper
- Salt

Directions:

1. Press the sauté button on the Instant Pot, then heat the oil in it.
2. Add the onion and cook it for 2 min.
3. Add the remaining ingredients except for the cheese, then put on the lid and cook for 9 min on high pressure.
4. Once the time is up, use the quick method to release the pressure.
5. Stir in the cheese until it melts, then serve warm and enjoy.

Cheesy Hot Enchiladas

(Prep Time: 15 min | Cooking Time: 44 min |
Servings 4)

Ingredients:

- 1 ½ pound of chicken breasts

- 12 corn tortillas
- 16 ounces of tomato sauce
- 8 ounces of Monterey jack cheese, shredded
- 8 ounces of cheddar cheese, shredded
- 1 cup of yellow onion, diced
- 1 cup of chicken broth
- 2 tablespoons of chili powder
- 1 tablespoon of oil
- 1 jalapeno, seeded and minced
- 1 teaspoon of cumin
- 1 teaspoon of sugar
- 3 cloves of garlic, minced
- Black pepper
- Salt

Directions:

1. Press the sauté button on the Instant Pot, then heat the oil in it.
2. Add the onion, jalapeno and garlic and cook for 4 min.
3. Stir in the tomato sauce with chicken breasts, chili powder, broth, chili powder, cumin, sugar, some salt and pepper.
4. Put on the lid and cook for 12 min on high pressure.
5. Once the time is up, use the natural method to release the pressure.
6. Drain the chicken breasts and shred them.
7. Preheat the oven to 400 F.

8. Place the tortillas on a lined baking sheet and brush both sides with oil.
9. Spoon ¼ of the chicken sauce from the pot into a greased baking dish.
10. Spread half of the enchilada sauce on the tortillas, then top with the shredded chicken and half of the cheese. Then roll the tortillas.
11. Place the enchiladas in the baking dish, then spread the remaining sauce over them.
12. Sprinkle the cheese on top and cook them in the oven for 28 min.
13. Once the time is up, serve your enchiladas warm and enjoy.

Mouth Watering Chocolate Chip Breakfast Pancakes

(Prep Time: 15 min | Cooking Time: 20 min | Servings 4)

Ingredients:

- 2 cups all purpose flour
- 2 1/2 tsp baking powder
- 2 tbsp granulated white sugar

- 2 large eggs
- 1 1/2 cups milk

Directions:

1. In a large mixing bowl, whisk together eggs and milk until completely blended. Add in remaining ingredients and whisk again.
2. Thoroughly grease the interior of your instant pot with cooking oil spray. Pour in batter.
3. Seal lid with vent closed and program instant pot to manual mode. Set pressure to low pressure and cook for 45 minutes. If you want something a little less crispy, you may want to try a few less minutes. If your Instant Pot gives an overheating error, you can also try to set it to rice mode instead of manual, low pressure, 45 minutes, which seems to solve the issue.
4. Check on the cake when the Instant Pot indicates it's done cooking. If you cake is not quite done, let it continue to cook on low pressure for a few more minutes.
5. Use a spatula to further loosen cake from the sides of the pan. Very carefully, pop the cake out upside down so that the bottom is now the top.
6. Serve with your favorite pancake toppings

Zesty Broccoli and Shrimp Risotto

(Prep Time: 15 min | Cooking Time: 20 min |
Servings 4)

Ingredients:

- 1 pound of shrimp, divided and peeled
- 3 ½ cup of chicken broth
- 1 ½ cup of arborio rice
- 1 cup of broccoli florets, finely chopped

- ½ cup of dry white wine
- ½ cup of parmesan cheese
- ½ yellow onion, finely chopped
- 2 tablespoons of fresh lemon juice
- 1 tablespoon of butter
- 1 tablespoon of parsley, finely chopped
- 2 teaspoons of olive oil
- Black pepper
- Garlic
- Salt

Directions:

1. Press the sauté button on the instant Pot and heat 1 teaspoon of olive oil in it.
2. Cook the onions for 2 min.
3. Stir in the garlic with broccoli then cook them for another 2 min.
4. Combine the butter with the rice and stir for 1 min.
5. Combine the cheese with wine, broth, and some salt and pepper.
6. Replace the lid and cook for 9 min on high pressure.
7. Once the time is up, use the natural method to release the pressure.
8. Push the risotto to the side of the pot using the back of a spoon, then press the sauté button.
9. Pour the remaining 1 teaspoon of oil in the empty side, then sauté the shrimp for 5 min.

10. Once the time is up, stir in the lemon juice, then serve your risotto warm and enjoy.

Pork Stew

(Prep Time: 15 min | Cooking Time: 20 min | Servings 4)

Ingredients:

- 1 pound of pork loin, diced
- 3 yellow onions, finely chopped
- 2 cups of beef stock
- 14.5 ounces of tomato, diced
- 2 red bell peppers, seeded and diced

- 3 carrots, shredded
- 1 cup of water
- 4 tablespoons of canola oil
- 2 tablespoons of paprika
- 2 rosemary stick
- 2 tablespoons of tomato paste
- 4 cloves of garlic, minced
- 3 bay leaves
- Black pepper
- Salt

Directions:

1. Press the sauté button on the Instant Pot, then heat the oil in it.
2. Sauté the vegetables with the garlic for 5 min.
3. Stir in the remaining ingredients, then put on the lid and cook for 30 min on high pressure.
4. Once the time is up, use the natural method to release the pressure.

Conclusion

Thank you again for checking out this book! I really do hope you found the recipes as tasty and mouthwatering as I did, and most importantly, I hope you enjoyed cooking it!

Printed in Great Britain
by Amazon